Unhistorical

AKRON SERIES IN POETRY

AKRON SERIES IN POETRY
Mary Biddinger, Editor

Brittany Cavallaro, *Unhistorical*
Tyler Mills, *Hawk Parable*
Caryl Pagel, *Twice Told*
Emily Rosko, *Weather Inventions*
Emilia Phillips, *Empty Clip*
Anne Barngrover, *Brazen Creature*
Matthew Guenette, *Vasectomania*
Sandra Simonds, *Further Problems with Pleasure*
Leslie Harrison, *The Book of Endings*
Emilia Phillips, *Groundspeed*
Philip Metres, *Pictures at an Exhibition: A Petersburg Album*
Jennifer Moore, *The Veronica Maneuver*
Brittany Cavallaro, *Girl-King*
Oliver de la Paz, *Post Subject: A Fable*
John Repp, *Fat Jersey Blues*
Emilia Phillips, *Signaletics*
Seth Abramson, *Thievery*
Steve Kistulentz, *Little Black Daydream*
Jason Bredle, *Carnival*
Emily Rosko, *Prop Rockery*
Alison Pelegrin, *Hurricane Party*
Matthew Guenette, *American Busboy*
Joshua Harmon, *Le Spleen de Poughkeepsie*

Titles published since 2010.
For a complete listing of titles published in the series,
go to www.uakron.edu/uapress/poetry.

Unhistorical

Brittany Cavallaro

The University of Akron Press
Akron, Ohio

ISBN: 978-1-629221-08-3 (paper)
ISBN: 978-1-629221-09-0 (ePDF)
ISBN: 978-1-629221-10-6 (ePub)

Library of Congress Cataloging-in-Publication Data
Names: Cavallaro, Brittany, author.
Title: Unhistorical / Brittany Cavallaro.
Description: First edition. | Akron, Ohio : The University of Akron Press, 2019. |
  Series: Akron series in poetry |
Identifiers: LCCN 2018051839 (print) | LCCN 2018055292 (ebook) | ISBN
  9781629221090 (ePDF) | ISBN 9781629221106 (ePub) | ISBN 9781629221083
  (paperback :alk. paper)
Subjects: LCSH: American poetry—21st century.
Classification: LCC PS3603.A89895 (ebook) | LCC PS3603.A89895 A6 2019 (print)
  | DDC 811/.6—dc23
LC record available at https://lccn.loc.gov/2018051839

Cover image: *Thicket*, © Suzanne Moxhay. Used with permission. Cover design by Amy
Freels.

Unhistorical was designed and typeset in Baskerville by Amy Freels and printed on sixty-pound natural and bound by Bookmasters of Ashland, Ohio.

Produced in conjunction with the
University of Akron Affordable Learning
Initiative. More information is available
at www.uakron.edu/affordablelearning/

CONTENTS

Pastiche with Lines from Conan Doyle   1

I. Edinburgh, 2008
Your Twenties   5
Leitmotif   6
After Image   7
Portraiture   8
"Tell Me What You Want from Me"   9
Folly   10
Forever   12
Orphic Hymn   13
A Gate   14
We Didn't See It at First, but
    After That We Saw It All the Time   15
National Health Service   16
Evidence   17
Portions   18
Self-Portrait as John Watson   19

II. The Resurrectionists: London, 1896
Watson's Diary (i)   23
Holmes Gives a Demonstration of His Methods   24
from The Adventure of the Hooded Woman   26
221b Baker Street, in Repose   27
Self-Portrait as Black MoodBrown Study   28
from The Adventure of the Hooded Woman   29
Watson's Diary (ii)   30
from The Adventure of the Hooded Woman   31
Self-Portrait as Morocco Case   32
Watson Takes a Client in Holmes's Absence   33

Holmes, on Relief   35
Performance   36
Self-Portrait as "The Final Problem"   38
Holmes, on Spiritualism   39
Watson's Diary (iii)   40
Holmes, on Withdrawal   41
Watson's Diary (iv)   42

III. Milwaukee, 20—

Love Poem   45
Unhistorical   47
Exceptions   48
Games   50
At the Wisconsin State Fair   51
Salad Days   52
Relationship with Textiles and Barter   53
Five Years Later   54
Not a Question   55
Apologia   56
His Last Bow, 1919   57
Redux   58
Self-Portrait as Sherlock Holmes   59

Acknowledgments   61

Come at once if convenient. If inconvenient come all the same.

SIR ARTHUR CONAN DOYLE

PASTICHE WITH LINES FROM CONAN DOYLE

Milwaukee, 2012

I have pinpointed the particular flaw
        in our relations: it's how you transpose
    each small riot into sadness but have
no Stradivarius to mourn on——you have my ears,

        and my feet freeze in our bed,
     and the knocking in the night is
just a dear friend looking to score, our cat
        is named for a knave. We tweak

     our epaulets, we make margaritas
in rooms populated by the ephemera
        of other lives that I cannot shore up
    my own against. This fashion rag

tells me to think of the highlands
        so I eye-drop water into my Laphroaig
   and when later, for work, I stand
on the Scottish street on which I once lived,

      it is blue melodrama or it is
    not real, and if the stories tally
I'll watch it again on the plane. This may appeal
      to your lurid taste in fiction,

   darling: I am your constant companion,
and we have never both lived within these same walls.

I.

Edinburgh, 2008

YOUR TWENTIES

The framed art creeps along the wall, the cat
        wants another cat, you make bowls that I eat from—
I could eat, since your ask always comes at four.

The plants outside grow. They tumble down
        to the water, wanting water. I wake up
in your arms. I remember not to look back

when leading a man out of darkness. A girl outside
        asks me, *do you know where* and then blanches
sudden as the morning. Years ago

I lived in a city built onto itself. Each street
        ate its own tail. When I marry you
I am making a promise. A mirror bought isn't bought alone.

LEITMOTIF

The ghost wants to walk through
your bedroom wall. *When do you sleep?*
The ghost wants to know. It wants to turn
the faucet on for your morning shower.
It's helping. It fills your French press. The water
turns out red. The ghost isn't sure how
to fix that. Your nightgown is cotton, the kind
the ghost likes. The ghost reaches for your hem
like a cat would. If it were a cat, the ghost
could warm your ankles. It could make
the walking easier. The ghost doesn't like it
when you go back to bed. The ghost opens
your shutters all at once because it's morning.
Why are you sleeping? The dust the ghost leaves
is white like a drug or a lime deposit. The taps
are still turned on. The ghost lets them wash
your tiles clean. It would kiss your face clean
like a cat, if you'd let it. The ghost would come
into your bed and stop your wild hands. Its hands
are what matter. Your comforter has weight.
If it spreads itself above you like a quilt,
you might feel it. The ghost wants you to feel it
again. The ghost has made a lake
of itself. You can take it into your lungs.

AFTER IMAGE

In one take, the blue ruck of the night was
        a cataract cloud. Through the shades, my bad eye
strained at a light the other couldn't see. The world

    was often split this way, and I, unsurprised,
        ate fig-and-rose cookies on a Saturday,
burned your letters the next. When I fell down the stairs,

    you red-taped their ends without my asking
        but then swore at your ruined fingers.
Yes, the traffic in the mornings and the traffic

    at night, and you, avid in your glasses,
        the men in your biographies,
their terrible crimes. Our love kept me here

    against my will. When my right side clouded
        like a mirror, as I'd been told by my doctors
it would, I woke in tubing and tape

    to too much light. In my paper gown,
        I asked, cotton-mouthed, for a chocolate,
and you said, *you can't have one,* then *open your mouth.*

PORTRAITURE

In this drawing, the girl hides behind herself. The sun is too much
        in her hands. In this drawing, the girl's double
    wears green around her hair, a decision made

to tell them apart. To be so lucky. To remember a night with him—
        here's a string, he said, pulling it between his hands.
    With her butter knife he frayed its ends, then peeled the red line

away from itself. At the end of a black hole's endlessness,
        every present layered onto itself. Shift one, and another shifts,
    his hand returns to the light switch. Here, in her studio, the artist

wears a long braid down each shoulder. She glances at the window,
        at her reflection laid out against the street's bright leaves—
    both here, for now, though all the paintings look away.

"TELL ME WHAT YOU WANT FROM ME"

I told him. An apartment with no doors
and crown molding where I'd teach him
how to be alone. Third and King, masked
and bare, beloved and yet left by himself
with the uncovered furniture and the fire.
A loosening finger, a snap-case
of yellowed pages and him,
                            when I wanted him
(Apollonian, twenty-five), his head lolled back
against the sheets we wouldn't clean. We'd ash
on the floor. I could want while I still had
what I wanted: no novelty, just flush-
ruined, him pleading like a child. In the caverns
beneath, I would enter an alcove and there
my tabernacle. Tea brewed from the ash
of letters sent by other swains, swan-necked
photos (me alone in the garden). My shadow
pinned down and stitched again to my feet.

FOLLY

A building that has no purpose except as an ornament.

My thinking was
        the hedgerows, manicured,
on the manicured drive to the ruin.

I spun it so the taut line
        of you in the seat beside
was a favor to me. Your sulks I had loved

for their tenacity, and you
        for your disdain
of Baroque composers and dictionaries

and all but the very worst
        television, the plainest girls,
of most things but me. I could do nothing

with you in this way.
        On that English hill I counted
the nine pillars of a would-be Parthenon

and you kicked a rock
        across the field. *A pity,* you said,
what you find beautiful. Through your lips

the gap in your teeth.
        I could never help, as it wasn't
what you wanted. I couldn't make bricks

without clay, and the design's
       missing pages, and the structure
spoke to itself at night. And still people came

    in their mud boots and corduroys,
       with their cameras, aloud
they wondered how this began—stone dragged

    from the earth to appease
       some small god
that refused them, and was forgotten.

FOREVER

It wasn't so hard to want it, while the ancient stove smoked
      and our friends slept under their coats
            on the linoleum. The door's warped wood

      meant it never shut completely, so each snap of wind

masked my movement toward you on the sofa. We hadn't kissed,
      wouldn't—we both had partners—I undid
            my hair from its braids and shook it out

      over my burning shoulders. Our friends woke. They read

tarot on the floor; someone tuned a guitar, another broke down
      some boxes and threw them on the fire. My suitcase
            was brought in and dismembered,

      and my green party dress, and the table where I'd drafted

a letter home, of which there was then a staged reading. I was told
      I could direct my own production, as there was time.
            There was time for me to move myself so minutely

that I would never reach you. I could have what I wanted.
      The impossibility, the creeping forward all the same.

ORPHIC HYMN

I didn't want to be touched. I wanted to be held
in the grip of something I couldn't escape. I wanted

to run straight back into the forest, wanted him
to forget the black guitar. I had always been that girl

except for the days I couldn't climb from my bed.
No matter. In the song, he sang, *I am the thing*

that ate the flowers. Then he smiled with his straight teeth.
In the song the long forest path changed with every turn—

I saw meadows in the hard red earth. Behind me
he played the instrument I'd bought only for display.

A GATE

It originates at the detail,
the hinge of the door
to the museum. Not the landscape
or the figure that might be
art, might be a coin-collector,
maybe both. How you've taken us
to twenty such places
in the name of teaching me.
The titles were always better
than their canvases, all that
blank sincerity. Their voices—
if voiced—would spiral up
into sincerity, and I never
liked a sound for what it signified.
I lost you in the impressionists.
Found the gate to the pleasure-garden
behind the museum. There, I named
no flowers, no birds. Let the world
be a worse sketch, left untitled.

WE DIDN'T SEE IT AT FIRST, BUT AFTER THAT WE SAW IT ALL THE TIME

I said its syllables slowly over my cup like steam. Corrected your
   pronunciation.

I said of course not, I'm perfectly happy. The whole thing's covered in
   soot.

I said no, I didn't live there alone. I saw other people at market. My
   Swedish flatmate pinned
      a blanket to her wall, and I could stare at it when I was cold.

I said inflation, of course. And the bridges, so many, and it wasn't water
   running underneath.

I said I auditioned at least four before I made up my mind.

I said that we weren't ever seen without the other. I had my own room.
   It didn't change the story.

I said, stop. I said *here*, and *here*, and I circled your map.

NATIONAL HEALTH SERVICE

The nurse said *would you like to see,* said *he can hold your hand*
but if he did he would see what was on the screen,
what grew even in the seconds it took for him to cross

the room. We were sent back to wait where the girls *with*
were partitioned from the girls *without,* and in our corner
the girls were slim and nervous and all wore the same

suede boots. I added up my days left in Scotland, took away
my days left as a girl, watched the one beside me scrawl
her own name, *Georgia*, in interlocking letters down

the margins of her book. Her boots were brown,
had a slight heel, and her voice was Midlothian sweet
when she said *later.* I wore those boots; I wore tweed

because I was an educated girl, because I could be from
any titled house, I let my boyfriend answer the questions,
widened my eyes to look *delicate*, the word the nurse used

to describe my mother's necklace, a comfort
after I vomited in the sterile sink. I didn't speak—
my vowels were broad, my *okays* cheerful

no matter how I said them. I said them in my head.
She gave me a form to fill out in triplicate, and when
the pen wouldn't bleed through, I wrote my name again

and again and again, I would write it anywhere
if it meant I didn't have to keep it.

EVIDENCE

four plates before we had three   and the tumbler
from Edinburgh I slipped   your new tie pin

into   held the glass above one eye
like a dirty fish   anyway it was the dish rack   wet

I pressed my fist to my mouth   your hands
cut your lips thinned   my own feet were bare

you said   *you're crying*   like I'd fallen and spilled
into little tinsels of gold   delighted   my mother handing

me ceramic foxes   salt cellars   scalloped plates
too small to eat on   she saw the basement flat I'd taken

alone or I'd been   well I wrapped myself in paper
lanterns   I had it all for years I hadn't   couldn't

because I knew how it was done   some afternoon
wet hands and us   so poor your red misery   eye-dropped

into every glass of water   extravagant like wine I ate
I kept my head   through rolling heat   blood cylindered

and sold   the summer nothing unfurled from its homes
until   what was one plate, one cup   you eyeing me   satisfied

a fork pulling at the piece before you   is it done   is it done

PORTIONS

The wolves we met were French and they sharpened
   their teeth on stones, and they had
beautiful restaurants, and each of them fed us

 in turn. And you were you, in this dream,
   but you were pleased when I began
to pack my things—you rolled the stone back from our cave

 and I woke, and my flight was on time. I made
   breakfast. The wind stripped rocks
from Arthur's Seat, and below us the market

 did a brisk trade in disposables. I had a dream
   where you bound my wrists in expensive rope
below a symbol for love, and that symbol too

 stood for the trees that shook in pairs, or singly,
   and some didn't shake at all.
And I was awake through it, and I held the stove

 for balance. You turned from the game and loped
   to me like a wolf, in your Ramones shirt
and ripped-up jeans, a Scottish prince bent on

 halving me. I could stay, I knew, only if I could go;
   then you'd have what parts you wanted
before my body was mixed with ash, and salted.

SELF PORTRAIT AS JOHN WATSON

If it's to me to write the story, I will be master
of my subject. So be the gleaming machine

for my sake. Take the facts of these years

and show me how, like lovers,
they betray us. If I were the logician, I'd say

I wrote you wrong so you stayed mine.

II.   The Resurrectionists
London, 1896

For years the author has, in his own domestic circle, obtained inspired messages through the hand and voice of his wife, which have been of the most lofty and often of the most evidential nature. They are, however, too personal and intimate to be discussed in a general survey of the subject.

The History of Spiritualism, Sir Arthur Conan Doyle

WATSON'S DIARY (i)

Singular experience at the track. H. sent me
there as witness to the end. Our man now
in chains. Pocketed a crop, two sovereigns.
The first because I am a sentimental man.
Gave five shillings to the girl for her part,
her ashy hair like my poor Mary's.

At the top of the stairs I had to gather myself.
Counted the vials in the drawer. Seven.
Dreamt of teeth, the long mouth stretched
over the gate. H. by the fire when I retired,
again when I woke.

No letters today.

HOLMES GIVES A DEMONSTRATION OF HIS METHODS

If the dun horse is old and still water-glossy,
then arsenic was given, enough to cover

a knife's blade. If you look in its mouth
then it will die three days hence. If the lady places

a man's bet, then her skirts will show the result
as a skirt shows mud from a dog-cart.

She will loiter across our street. Her cape
of course is white. Then my good friend

will observe her from our window
as he observes his breakfast or my morocco case

and its needle. If the letter asking for my assistance
does not arrive, I will open the case.

There is medicine within. This is a fault
but I keep what information I find

necessary. My friend knows medicine
as he knows his soul. His service revolver

is in the locked drawer. Some mornings
I hear each of his widower's gasps

clear as the clap of the gate
behind the jockeys. I can hear this

even before he wakes. If he strikes
a match off his chin then he has not shaved

this week. If no letter arrives
then there is a solution.

from THE ADVENTURE OF
THE HOODED WOMAN

My previous experience accompanying my constant companion had not adequately prepared me for the depraved situation upon which Sherlock Holmes had stumbled. It was the summer of '95, and we had few cases at that moment; some rather embarrassing business with the French ambassador had just been straightened out, but the situation had so overtaken Holmes's time that he had turned away a surfeit of clients just before his culprit more or less placed himself in my dear friend's exacting hands. We celebrated. We slept. The sun set. Then the girl in white at the window, then at the door, then pleading, bent-kneed, at my friend's unworthy feet. I stood with my notebook: *small white shoes, buttoned at the ankle.* She could not, or would not, open her pink mouth. This is what I am prepared to tell you: a fortnight found us bedded down in a Berkshire stable. A duke's fists full of needles. The cellar below our feet filled with the dying girls sunk down in their skirts. I could not know. I thought neither of us could. Each horse a renowned runner. Her mouth had bled for weeks.

221B BAKER STREET, IN REPOSE

Alphabetized detritus. A ship half-built
      in a brief, clean circle and beside it
a reliquary of criminal teeth. Two books

      of eschatology that the detective will not
study, that his friend secrets beneath

his sheets. He sleeps upstairs. His bad leg
      slams each third step. The desk downstairs
and a tangled clutch of horsehair that refuses

      its bow. The Stradivarius upstairs, then down,
then laid at a right angle to the initials shot

into the wall. Twelve bullets above the side-
      board. A waxwork bust of the detective,
wounded, and the curtains that cannot conceal

      the scorch marks. A tea service and sandwiches.
A pince-nez and six pairs of sideburns, one

flame-red, two blonde. They wait in the drawer
      with the morocco case. It waits, like his dinner,
for his friend to appear. Without his wife

      he has no excuse. The detective scratches
on his chalkboard and arrives at

a known quantity. The stairs are beyond that, and the laughter
      in the tin box, the seizure-scrabble
of what's underneath it.

SELF PORTRAIT AS BLACK MOOD/ BROWN STUDY

Still by accident and not design.
The bare desk a problem. The library
a problem of arrangement. A container
spilled if too still, and the page
a problem too, the days spent
in pencil, tracing someone else's words
for pay, and the empty afternoon,
bare in its branches but still outside
the glass. And I am in. I am making
something from the cords of it,
the knots and bows, the leather that seizes
when wet, will tie it tightly enough
to resist my weight and make it
turn, the thought facing thought,
the domestic yawn, the lean and problem
the source of the problem. The self
the problem, presented as solution.

from THE ADVENTURE OF THE HOODED WOMAN

My previous experience accompanying my constant companion had not adequately prepared me for the depraved situation upon which Sherlock Holmes had stumbled. Much later, when the two of us were in our cups, he would blame the entirety of the mess on my propensity to watch the pretty parasoled girls out the window. *You see, Doctor, but you do not observe,* he said, bowing wretchedly away at his violin. It was the summer of '95, and we had few cases at that moment; some rather embarrassing business with the French ambassador and his rosebush of a daughter had just been straightened out, but the situation had so overtaken Holmes's time that he had turned away a surfeit of clients just before his culprit more or less placed himself in my dear friend's exacting hands. Then? A fortnight of death; another of silence. Indeed, a single day of Holmes taking that most abhorrent cure—the black moods in which he cursed every petty aristocrat by exact indiscretion before he lapsed into a twitching silence punctuated only by his gnawing at his raw lower lip—that is to say, I passed long hours at my club. I became a rather dab hand at euchre. I saw her still: the beautiful girl in the street, her dusty skirts, the shock of leather in her mouth.

WATSON'S DIARY (ii)

Not left the flat. The Hooded Woman, Or: Her Last Run. (Meaning the horse.) Four cross-outs. When completed the account will be short. H. betrays no interest, not an eyelid's worth. While I write, he stabs the pen-knife into the mantle and the letters beneath are further destroyed. Six vials now.

A full week since our last. The morocco case open atop the drawer, the solution mixed beside. Argument. Citrus ices ordered for our dinner. Not by my request. The table is too small for this misery. Hotpot then billiards at the club. Pocketed ten shillings. Cannot find a proper place for the crop. Bedside table suggests it is unimportant. Sitting room suggests it is a fair topic for conversation.

H. handles his bow as if it were a bell-pull. The violin sounds ill. If I were to diagnose, would suggest oil of violet and perhaps a bath. H.? Cocaine and sorting through the ash trap again. All this burning.

Singular. Today at tea H. praised my memoirs while studying my fingernails. I could hide nothing from him even if I wanted to do so. How I hid my Mary from him. How I should have taken her away.

from THE ADVENTURE OF
THE HOODED WOMAN

I'll say that I developed a fair amount of skill propping
bruised men against myself, but my God, your wasted
mouth. Later, when the two of us were in our cups, you
would blame the entirety of the mess on my propensity to
stare at you across the room. *You see, Doctor, but you do not
observe,* you said, sliding the needle behind a shaking hand.
It was the summer of '95, and we had few cases after that
rather embarrassing business between the French ambassador
and his filly of a daughter—you naturally had straightened
the situation out before I came home from the track. The
girls there like spit and grease. Send me on an errand to the
horses again and I could conceivably mouth the pistol myself.
Your exacting hands. Then? A fortnight of silence. Indeed,
a single day of your black moods, the women sussed out
down to boot size, to brain, your evident hatred, the
twitching silence, the hawker's punctuation, you gnawing
and gnawing at your raw lower lip—that is to say, I passed
long hours at my club. I became a rather dab hand at the
cold. And then that beautiful girl in the street, like some
blessedly silent memory—all I had now three years past—
her dusty fingers, the shock of love in her mouth. I am a
kind man. You cannot be the last thing in this world for me.

SELF PORTRAIT AS MOROCCO CASE

Locked in the drawer with your pocketbook,
     a pen. A knife inside fashioned from glass, steel
to a point—I've hidden myself like a ration

     or the obvious path to the armistice. Under
the mattress where you sleep, I breathe.
     If I am your timepiece and the needle

that stitches your nights together. There is no
     distraction like this, the one that undoes you
in the way the wrong words can't, you won't

     undo the resolute—that insistence
in the blood, the drop as logical as love.

WATSON TAKES A CLIENT IN HOLMES'S ABSENCE

The detective has panted and paced for days,
refused food, wrapped his red-tracked arms

around the doctor's legs, begged with his mouth.
Sedated, he sleeps, and so the doctor is alone,

a small white glove to his nose. The things
he can touch still dwindle in their numbers.

Under the influence of such monomania,
a man could be capable of any fantastic outrage.

The lost heat of his wife like gas-light. He could,
after grinding his teeth into paste, allow himself

to follow a fancy. Could allow in the visitor
for the detective, could call *himself* the detective,

Dr. Holmes, throw out his arms, hawk-like, and sneer
at the lady in the door. He is surprised to find

this so easy, the curt greeting, his own knowing
hands waving her in. In the next room

Holmes whispers in his sleep. The lost wife then becomes
a tightened belt. Becomes a client. It could be

this girl. Could be the next. This girl naturally carries
a set of smart gloves and a letter from the medium

Lady Jean. There could be a brother or a fiancé,
an assurance that his form will be projected onstage.

She could beg this wavering Holmes,
show him her beloved's hair in a locket

she proffers from her pale fist. She could say
I loved. Compliment his moustache and brush

a curl from her eyes. The curl could be
blonde. Could list away down her face. His wife.

This Mary. Asks for an escort to a séance
at a prominent address. Edinburgh. The city

of his birth. She could say something
about coffins or the lost. The wife then

a losing horse. A hand seizing after an idea.

HOLMES, ON RELIEF

I make it my business to know
where things are kept. The brother
in the goose-yard, bald and praying,
agitating each fowl, wanting
the precious stone no longer
in its crop. Why would he keep it
in a safe? Would a man, having framed
his wife, lean against the piano-forte
as she sang for him? The birds dashing
against the lighted window. These wives,
on the endless train to their ailing mothers
or in the dark cavern of their comfortable rooms.
In the dark of their underground boxes, Watson,
not thrust into the tea-lights of an ossified hag
and her wet, lying mouth. The dead
cannot come back to us. What medium
do you require for your relief? Come here.
Are you a medical man? Do you believe
in this science? There are faster ways
to exhaustion. I have trained, swift-fisted,
with the lofted leather bag,
with the needle. The flexed arm
and jab. What has already passed
through you—Afghan bullets,
your diaphanous days, spirits
like sherry or wine? I make a practice
of keeping. What do I keep in myself?
Where do you keep your arms?

PERFORMANCE

Once she is exposed

Edinburgh's streets are like the hands in a pocket-watch.

we will leave. I am not yours

To promise an image of her brother in the silver bowl.

to command in this or any thing,

Nothing appears. The audience requires more faith to keep

Holmes. Of course I will stand

those milliner's mistakes on their heads. If nothing else

if my wife's name is spoken, I am not

you wear my own flapped cap convincingly, though

a fool. Yes, I carry her glove

on that stage you are as bare as her moon-face.

in my own. I cannot brook further refusals—

To stroke your hands? To hold a tallow candle

I give over every last one

to your eyes? You must begin seeing your clients in this theater.

to your performative kindness

The alphabetic women extra-sensed in this room.

and all you want is to tally up

How many will you 'yes'? I rather doubt

my loyalty, which is to say my silence,

you yearn to hear of where they watch you.

which is to say you know

They died for want of you.

your simpering Boswell

For your second bedroom. Your second seat

saws away at this farce

by our fire. Their white-ash eyes—their hair pale as burning, you are
   quite fond

so I may ignore how

of the dainty ones. So our medium cannot give us

I am responsible—

a body. My dear Watson, will you step down?

she sees through me like the Water of Leith

SELF-PORTRAIT AS "THE FINAL PROBLEM"

Gave a stranger your coat, gave another your legs,
          walked away when the man you loved
     loved someone who could wake up

          before him. You were lazy, at best.
At best, the lights jangled like a set of silent keys,
          and the cover on the mirror hid the person

     you had no choice but to be. You burnt down
          your house, lived there another year.
Burnt down your city and refused to seed

          the ashes for a garden. Your face blushed quick-
     lime when spring came, but by definition
the beautiful is useless; the waterfall, frozen;

          you'll lead us to our true hearts
     and none of us will come back.

HOLMES, ON SPIRITUALISM

A sitting room is not the proper setting
for a spiritual awakening. As a horse forgets
his shoes (he is not, after all, the one to nail them
to his feet), so can a man forget his deceased wife
despite previous adoration. Adoration: the sudden
attention to such details (unbrushed coat, needle-
mark in the crook of an arm) in a lady's appearance
when these have not been marked before
in one's closest companion. When you assumed
my death, you quit me after a quarter hour.
I have trained you well in observation
and distance. There are certain
well-carved tables, excellent china,
there are vessels for the quiet governesses
of tragic good breeding who are pleased to rise
from the dead and come back to their husbands
for a justifiable fee.
                    Come back. See, I am fond
of charlatans. There is a certain amount of pleasure
in disguise and the caught-breath escape
from water and chains. The drowning
or how it is imagined. If you had been watching closely?
Then I could have returned sooner. Here I will differentiate
between legerdemain and what meager love
I have witnessed. What desire, to call back
the dead to watch you take your tea.

WATSON'S DIARY (iii)

.

If singularity added to a thing's value. Many
Marys, so mine is nothing. Perhaps I thought
that, with so many seeming likenesses, surely
I could have her again. In the window-seat,
laughing over a red-backed book, too
absorbed to see me standing there. In a city
this size I thought, surely there is another
window, another wife. H. would not be
surprised. There was, after all, another of
him.

He could be my shadow-self, if that shadow
were also a dug hole.

Naturally the girl did not glimpse her brother
on that stage though I confess I left before
its conclusion. Still remittance will come by
post, I am sure of it. What H. commands,
even when he is not himself.

On the train back to London, the man in
my compartment not a vicar. Naturally. Yet
I let him believe I did not know until, with
a flourish, H. peeled off gloves, moustache.
Consuetudinis magna vis est. I averted my eyes
for decency's sake.

HOLMES, ON WITHDRAWAL

I watch as if I've taken the aft seat
in our carriage—what is past
retreats from me, while the next town
sharpens only for you. Customarily
our nation progresses toward more
and better punishment; we did once agree
to take digs together. To ensure my mistake,
I lift the floorboard beneath your bed
to retrieve the vial I once allowed you
to find, I inject that as well. Make nothing of her miniature
that you hid away with my medicine. Make nothing
of this Mendelssohn while I watch you decide whether
to leave me. My dear, I play the Mendelssohn
as an apology you'd no doubt refuse
if you saw it as such. I play the Tchaikovsky
I abhor for the lost girls in Reading,
keeping time with the earth, and the Verdi you love
for the men they will never have, men
with well-trimmed moustaches, medical bags,
men with whom I have no sympathy. Then a gypsy air
to prolong the evening, to stave off want,
and hunger, to stop your lips from mourning
what I left you at that cliff to mourn. Let them
be lips again. After, the Bach. And then the Brahms
because you loved it once, and with the pleasure
in repetition, you could perhaps love it again.

WATSON'S DIARY (iv)

All these stories, as if for children. In the
logbook, their given names before their
pseudonyms. Black Pearl, Danceless, Red-
briar, Hooded Girl. What I do not sell to the
Strand: all those women piled like useless
data. *Where were their husbands then?* Those
were his words. He toed one with a black
boot. I retched in the corner, and then
followed him home.

I confess that day in Switzerland I felt some
measure of relief. How could I have known?
It took me years to pare out the last of him
with this dull knife. She could not know. She
thought it grief. What I felt was far too wild
to be that.

My own disappearance worth less, then. No
cliffs, no consumption. The men will move
my things to my practice, and I will be of
some good. If, for want of me, he

No matter. I do not believe in such things.

III.

Milwaukee, 20—

LOVE POEM

In your childhood bed
    and in your cups—

when you think of me

am I abstracted? Is the pear white
    when in slivers?

Is the drawing quartered?
    Am I refusing again

to take off the last slip

I'd bought for tonight—
    I loved you most

in the next room,
    in the hallway.

A shower. The almost
    of you, without the eyes.

What if I wished it very much?

When I couldn't eat,
    paper nests, your smallest finger.

A girl edged up to
    every open window.

In the other story
    we kept the flat, the child.

I kept the rope in the shed.

In the other story where I didn't leave
    I left you.

Here. The beginning you wanted.

UNHISTORICAL

In this crepuscular era   of nowheres
    of clocks   miswound   Of no bows

when knots would do   Of a veil
      below a veil   I would never

lift   There is a night   where I find
     two photographs   of a night

we never spent   My flush the stutter
     even   in the still   As you mouth

some secret behind a hand   Strung light
    The lit tower   looming   like a trick

candle   This never happened
All the nights   I knew   were under

old blankets   Walking backward
    through security   A book

neither of us liked   in a bony chair
     The whole   in some rainy

curtained Thursday   I hold loose
   as I would some muscular version of you

the man I loved fey   Against the ending
     Against the factual one   This fiction of

   a place that wanted us

EXCEPTIONS

At first just birthdays,
Christmas. Then the two writers
we loved spoke together

in a museum. The old bird
hung above them, a guesswork. Then
the sweet shop closed. That one,

you said, made you dig out the photo.
Pretty enough for fairies. Fool even
the experts. But the costume store

shuttered. Then you took a course
on Wordsworth. The supporting actor
had your improbable freckles

so I sat up searching even
his commercials. Whenever you called
it said *Florida*. We laughed

but then the pictures of you smiling
on an American beach. Then
I had the date wrong. Then I ran out

of credit. What if it had never been open,
not once? Would we still claim
otherwise? My city never changed

owners. You'd left the old one
entirely. I had my doubts but you arrived,
part and parcel. We watched each other.

The flat walls wavered. They didn't know
what they could contain. At their edges
something receded. Something I couldn't see.

GAMES

Better at following rules than filling the blank seconds
between them. Say, the tire swing at midnight

in the Meadows you shouldn't cross, not alone. So
we'll never be. Say, should we, but if it's a question—

it's not. So fill a tin with medicine for your bedside
drawer. Say, no one's loved you like this. Doubtless.

You take it and make it art. With you, I can't insist
I'm worthless so there's a price. Your whispered laugh I love

but still the gestures make me nervous. I love
what—put it down, the declarations you've drawn

to exhibit for the camera. Cover my eyes, I think,
in pleasure. Count only to two, never higher.

AT THE WISCONSIN STATE FAIR

On the cable, our car shudder-swings
      as you sing to calm me—*we aren't here,*
        we aren't here in this rain, my orange shirt

      wet like failed lightning. The car beside

painted with faces of film stars, ducked
      and swollen as if drawn in a mirror.
        Watch, you say, as the ingénue tips away

      in the honest wind but, again, comes back.

You promise me your handful of tokens.
      You will live in this state less than a year.
        West Allis, sugarland, we have never been

      so in love as when we were elsewhere, Calton Hill,

the mountain undone and still shadowing
      the city below. We went there always on foot
        then coasted out, but our ride here halts midway.

      Beneath us, everything sells for the same price.

SALAD DAYS

We no longer created. We were still too young
to climb out into the darkened real houses.
I wanted it gone but you followed me
into the shower. There was some talk about sharing
our meals again, so long as we didn't feed
each other. I was full, so I pulled out the old contract
for our future. There would be two doors
and I could use neither. You would use these
for your work. We signed our names to the bottom;
this settled, we slept. Or you did. Or you didn't,
or we took turns, as we did then
because of the bombings, and I heard you
kneel as I lay awake. In the morning, our room
was white. I reminded you of iodine, the way I was
always ill. The light worked you clean like a blotter
but I was stained, and though I was stained
you tended my bed as one did in that house, in that time.

RELATIONSHIP WITH TEXTILES AND BARTER

You love me, and I watch the power lines outside
hang like the awning over a bazaar,

      where the wind is a salesman shaking each line

in front of our faces, our hands, the velvet ribbons
      that tie my dress together. *Come buy*

      the wind calls, but we have no fruit for trade

      though we offer both our winter-weight and
our sheets' cleanliness. We'll trade our bed

      for a library, and our library for girls tied up smart

with money, and those girls for two cocktails in a hotel bar
      and a contract saying we'll split our fieldstone evenly

      and no longer bring the other to the sharing table.

We share ourselves with ourselves, or, no, that's not right—
my with *mine*, I am the one who ties my ribbons tight.

FIVE YEARS LATER

I told myself, I want this, until I wanted it. And sometimes
my back lined up to the wall, and the wall loved me. In his chair

I toweled my hair, speaking quietly until I shouted
to see his eyes turn on. My fault lay between the lethargy

of habit, between the key in the lock and my hands in the bag.
Those storyless days with their smooth hours. In the way a person

becomes paper, I folded myself into an ear. No more last
names. No more nights out. And if I did this for myself, had I

wanted a nest built, like all nests, with my mouth and my teeth,
can I blame myself for it? Why would I then destroy what a man

was already so eager to take? I want this, I said to the mirror.
I ignored the ringing phone. My intact heart. I said it louder.

NOT A QUESTION

Tell the fire to bank. It does.

Ask the line to hold, keep it all
aloft just a breath

longer. Let the storm

kill the sheep. No one called
while you were out in the yard

shooting birds with one cocked

finger. Tell me
what coins belong in

the ash trap, which children

we should keep. How a love folds down
with some small coaxing.

APOLOGIA

I was always late. We kept reassurance
in your bedside drawer. I bought you
bespoke suits. I gave you an accordion,
leather goggles. Then we took it all off.
We built a fort and took it down
tenderly, snugly. I was late but you ran it
all the way to the mailbox. I was late
but they made me coffee in my border control
cell before they waved me through;
you, panting, held my visa. We had advocates,
not friends. Our friends had religion
about us together. I could stay three months.
I could stay but the police were involved,
the judges' chambers. We had a favorite
cartoon still. We had a secret password.
When I was thrown out, I took my own flat
and there, I used my sheets as sheets.
You could stay but it took three buses
and a ten-hour flight. You could stay but it cost
your next five years. When I left you
I laughed, then thought, *this is
unforgivable.* Then thought, *thank God.*

HIS LAST BOW, 1919

As we near the end of the story, we are told
that there are hills in this country, and while
they allow a certain amount of rise and fall
to the horses pulling the detective's trap,
these hills are not allowed to be beautiful, not
with their dirt clods and blue flowers;
not practical, either, though they conceal
his residence from the road with their
grassy overlap and swell. They are just hills,
as the detective's pocket watch is a device
that keeps what is left, despite its engraving
from his friend. If you have sorted through
what is necessary and all that remains is this,
the dirt, the flowers, the bees you keep
in your country house, alone—
that's what you must take to bed with you,
your beaten body and your revolver, there
more from love than habit. We receive
what we've wanted all these small years,
and still, at night, the bees spin thick
in their hives, and the man turns, and this is
the word, this was the only one still to write.

REDUX

Outside the surgical museum
a twenty-foot bone saw has oxidized,
is the color of the sea. I've given up

on an umbrella. Across South Bridge
a man who looks like you
is you, but since it's been years

I duck my head. In the city I've dreamt
myself into, it is never noon like it is now.
Your wrists catch the midday light

like scalpels or fieldstone—those stones
you tracked in running to the chemist, the oath
in your hand and then in my coat,

tattered, the midnight dress I wore
to our friends' weddings. The body beneath it
asleep. The clouds won't shift to show

what's beneath, but you are as constant
as the rain. I left, and so I'm in the crowd.
The light's not changed. I doubt it will.

SELF PORTRAIT AS SHERLOCK HOLMES

I am aware that in this performance

I star as myself. You place your scalpel in my hands
then take the appropriate number of steps

toward the door, through which enough light
shines in to illuminate my accumulated

soot. Yet they will remember me cat-clean.
When we return and rewind the mantle clock,

I begin again in my customary chair. Again
you will forget that you have married, that

the room is no longer yours. I can see
you fear it never was, and so with my mouth

I confirm it. Write again of my limits, the end,
the slow approach. In these rooms I carve out

other rooms; there, I litter as I'd like. Know that
I only direct what you set down. From these lines

I make my music.

ACKNOWLEDGMENTS

Thanks to the editors of the journals in which these poems first appeared, some in slightly different versions:

The Adroit Journal: "*from* The Adventure of the Hooded Woman (i)," "*from* The Adventure of the Hooded Woman (ii)" and "*from* The Adventure of the Hooded Woman (iii)"
AGNI: "Folly," "Forever"
Barrow Street: "Apologia," "Pastiche with Lines from Conan Doyle"
The Collagist: "Salad Days"
Colorado Review: "Five Years Later"
FourTwoNine: "Self-Portrait as John Watson," "Self-Portrait as Sherlock Holmes"
Great Lakes Review: "At the Wisconsin State Fair"
Iron Horse Literary Review: "Portions"
Meridian: "Relationship with Textiles and Barter"
Poetry Northwest: "After Image"
Salt Hill: "Your Twenties"
Spoon River Poetry Review: "Self Portrait as Morocco Case," "Sherlock Holmes Gives a Demonstration of His Methods"
The Southern Review: "Portraiture"
Subtropics: "Evidence"
TriQuarterly: "Leitmotif"

Thank you so much to the University of Akron Press, especially Mary Biddinger and Amy Freels, for believing in this project and in my work for so long. Thank you to Rebecca Dunham for her time and attention with these poems; you are an incredible mentor. Thanks, too, to Brenda Cardenas, Rebecca Hazelton, Richie Hofmann, Jacques J. Rancourt, and Corey Van Landingham for their careful readings and feedback. The Vermont Studio Center and the Rona Jaffe Foundation provided support and a beautiful space to write, and the National Endowment for the Arts gave me the gift of time to finish this manuscript; I am so grateful. Finally, thanks to my family for all their love, and to Chase, for everything.

Photo: Kit Williamson

Brittany Cavallaro is the author of *Girl-King*, which was an Editor's Choice for the Akron Poetry Prize and was published by University of Akron Press in 2015, as well as the *New York Times* bestselling author of the Charlotte Holmes series for young adults. Her poems have appeared in *AGNI*, *The Southern Review*, and *Tin House*, among other journals. She is the recipient of fellowships from the National Endowment for the Arts and the Vermont Studio Center, and scholarships from the Bread Loaf Writers Conference. She is an instructor of creative writing at the Interlochen Arts Academy.